THE GIRL ON THE SOFA

Jon Fosse

THE GIRL ON THE SOFA
(Jenta i sofaen)

in an English version by David Harrower

from a literal translation by
Neil Howard and Tonje Gotschalksen

OBERON BOOKS
LONDON

First published in 2002 by Oberon Books Ltd
521 Caledonian Road, London N7 9RH
Tel: +44 (0) 20 7607 3637 / Fax: +44 (0) 20 7607 3629
e-mail: info@oberonbooks.com
www.oberonbooks.com

Reprinted 2011

A catalogue record for this book is available from the British Library.

ISBN: 978-1-84002-326-8

Cover photography by Daniel Brinckmann

International New Writing and the Traverse Theatre

In 2001 *Jenta i sofaen*, a new play in Norwegian, was commissioned from Jon Fosse by the Traverse Theatre, Scotland. David Harrower's version, *The Girl on the Sofa*, was then commissioned by the Traverse under its international Playwrights in Partnership scheme (in association with the Paul Hamlyn Foundation).

Playwrights in Partnership was created by the Traverse in 2000 as part of the theatre's increased commitment to contemporary international playwrights alongside its development and championing of Scottish writers. The PiP scheme aims to improve the quality of performance translations of contemporary international drama. Each PiP commission matches an international playwright with their Scottish counterpart. The two playwrights are brought together in residency to work on a version of the play into Scots English (if necessary working with a literal translation), and the work's strength to date lies in the extensive involvement of the international playwright in the translation of their own play, paired with the skills of the Scottish partner playwrights as wordsmiths and dramatists.

The Girl on the Sofa was first performed on Monday 12 August 2002 by the Edinburgh International Festival in co-production with the Schaubühne am Lehniner Platz, Berlin.

Characters

WOMAN

GIRL

MAN

MOTHER

SISTER

UNCLE

SISTER OLDER

FATHER OLDER

FATHER

This version of *The Girl on the Sofa* was first performed by the
Edinburgh International Festival, in a co-production with the
Schaubühne am Lehniner Platz, Berlin, at the Royal Lyceum,
Edinburgh, on 12 August 2002. The cast included:

WOMAN, Ruth Lass
MAN, Paul M Meston
GIRL, Abby Ford
MOTHER, Julie Legrand
SISTER, Leah Muller
UNCLE, Daniel Cerqueira
SISTER OLDER, Liz Kettle
FATHER OLDER, Michael Mellinger

Director, Thomas Ostermeier
Designer, Rufus Didwidszus

Large, open, vaguely defined room. The walls made up of loose surfaces, of different sizes. Three of these are large unfinished paintings; the first shows the stern of a ship in turbulent seas; the second a man standing in the middle of a ship (he is much larger than the ship). The third and central painting is of a young girl sitting naked, with her feet drawn up, in the left-hand corner of a sofa. The other surfaces are ordinary walls with family photos, etc.

Behind the surfaces and in between them, in light and in the dark, still or moving, are the WOMAN, the SISTER, the MOTHER and the others.

A table and chairs in the middle, strongly lit.

A WOMAN, around fifty, moves from her place between the surfaces, proceeds hesitantly towards the middle, stops, turns towards the painting of the girl on the sofa, then moves forward, looks again at the painting.

WOMAN
No
(*Short pause.*)
it's so bad
(*Short pause.*)
I can't paint
Nobody's ever said I could of course
(*Short pause.*)
apart from me
so
maybe
I'm not sure
how it happened
(*Short pause.*)
I suppose I was sitting there
yes there on the sofa looking and looking
And then
(*She takes a paintbrush and goes and paints a little on the girl.*

The GIRL comes in, wearing briefs and shirt, sits in the left-hand corner of the sofa with her feet drawn up. The WOMAN returns to where she was, looks back at the picture.)
and you have to do something I suppose
When I was a child I'd draw
was good at drawing
But who isn't
Most children are good at drawing

GIRL

I'm quite good at drawing

WOMAN

So I suppose that's what happened
(*Short pause.*)
and so
yes
yes I suppose there was something I had to express
maybe
(*Short pause.*)
I saw a little girl today
she was walking along the road

GIRL

Today
what'm I going to do today

WOMAN

I suppose I wasn't very good at living
But you do live
And so
yes
yes in order to escape
in a way
maybe
yes
yes so I got the idea I should start to paint
And now I've painted
and painted
and painted
all these years

GIRL
I'm so bad at school
But I've a day off
And maybe
maybe I'll go into town

WOMAN
And you have to do something
And the pictures are big
fill room after room
(*Short pause.*)
Some of them I've destroyed
What else could I do
Pictures take up space
They're heavy
They take up all the space
there is
And when there's no space left
yes then you have to do something
with all the pictures
(*The WOMAN puts down the paintbrush, looks at the GIRL
sitting on the sofa.*)

GIRL
Maybe I can paint pictures

WOMAN
Ever since I was young
I've painted

GIRL
I'm good at drawing
(*Quite short pause.*)
and maybe I can paint pictures

WOMAN
And
yes
(*Short pause.*)
yes it feels like the pictures
inhabit everything

not because they're good
but because they're pictures
The colours in the pictures
they rise
and they
the colours
(*Short pause.*)
come towards me
now and then
anyway
they scare me
(*Short pause.*)
the colours come out of the picture
and they wrap around me
heavy
clinging
or light
and thin
like water

GIRL
What'm I going to do today

WOMAN
No
(*Short pause.*)
I can't paint
And I've stopped painting so many times
I have
I've stopped and stopped
And then I've started again
Not because it felt right
But you have to do something
And of course I've studied it
I've been learning how to paint
for many years
(*Short pause.*)
And I've
yes
well

I've exhibited in fact
as well
I have
and I've been part of
(*Cuts herself off.*)
yes some things have happened
but not that many
strictly speaking
in relation to everything I've painted
(*Short pause.*)
no
no actually almost nothing's happened
(*Pause.*)
I haven't sold one single picture
well maybe one
maybe
or
yes one picture
maybe
yes a long time ago

GIRL

Why's nothing
the way they say it is

WOMAN

And nobody wants my pictures
And it's easy to understand of course
because I can't paint
so why would anyone want to have
what I paint
(*The WOMAN goes back and looks at the picture.*)
No it's laughable
(*The MAN, around the same age as the WOMAN, comes in and walks towards her.*)

MAN

(*Looks at the picture.*)
It's nice

WOMAN
  No
  (*Short pause.*)
  it's bad
  (*Pause.*)

MAN
  I had a lot to do today

WOMAN
  Yes
  (*Short pause.*)

MAN
  You don't like the picture

WOMAN
  It's
  (*Cuts herself off.*)

MAN
  (*Continuing.*)
  the same as usual

WOMAN
  Yes
  (*Pause.*)
  I can't paint
  (*The WOMAN looks towards the MAN.*)
  Don't say you know
  (*The WOMAN laughs briefly.*)

MAN
  No no
  (*Pause.*)

WOMAN
  But

MAN
  Yes

WOMAN
  yes today

MAN
    Yes

WOMAN
    When I was out
    out shopping

MAN
    Yes

WOMAN
    I saw a little girl

MAN
    A little girl

WOMAN
    Yes
    yes I saw a little girl
    walking along the road

MAN
    Yes

WOMAN
    And she was walking so decisively
    so purposefully
    as if she was afraid
    but determined as well
    And she had a big rucksack on her back
    and the rucksack was half the size of her
    almost
    anyway
    And she had a hat on that was too big for her
    She was walking right on the edge of the road
    And the cars kept driving and driving past her
    And she was walking there right on the edge of the road
    She didn't look up
    I was walking towards her
    And then she saw me
    I could tell that she saw me
    (*The GIRL looks towards the WOMAN.*)
    And then she got scared

MAN
    Scared

WOMAN
    Yes I could tell she was scared
    she was scared because someone was coming towards her
    she started to walk more hesitantly
    but she walked on
    she made herself
    (*The GIRL looks down.*)
    She knew what she had to do
    She walked on
    (*Short pause.*)

MAN
    (*A little questioning.*)
    She was going to school

WOMAN
    Yes of course she was going to school
    It's a terrible way to go to school
    So many cars
    yes you know of course
    (*The MAN nods. Short pause.*)
    I can see her now
    Why's it like that
    Why do you see something
    and then you can't
    forget it

MAN
    It's just like that
    It happens to me too
    And maybe
    yes maybe it's like that
    something one sees
    can begin to mean
    so much
    somehow almost means much more than itself
    yes
    yes as if God

wants to say something by it
If he exists
(*Short pause.*)
None of that
I shouldn't be saying things like that
Can't you paint her

WOMAN
Then I'd be able to paint
but I can't paint
you know that of course

MAN
Yes and no

WOMAN
I can't paint
but I can see
and that's why
(*Cuts herself off.*)

MAN
Yes that you thought
you could paint

WOMAN
Yes
yes of course that's why
(*Pause.*)
Maybe she reminded me
yes that girl
of myself
when I was small
Or she reminded me
(*Cuts herself off.*)

MAN
Let's not talk about that

WOMAN
No
(*Pause.*)

MAN
> I'm tired

WOMAN
> Yes
> (*Pause. The MAN leaves and the WOMAN looks towards the GIRL.*)

GIRL
> And Mother's almost never at home
> And my Sister as well
> And Father's always away
> (*Pause.*)

WOMAN
> And now Mother's old
> She's going to die soon
> (*Short pause.*)
> I never had a child
> (*Short pause.*)
> And I'm getting old myself
> (*Short pause. The WOMAN sees the MOTHER come in wearing a dressing gown. The WOMAN picks up a paintbrush, continues painting the GIRL.*)

GIRL
> (*To the MOTHER.*)
> D'you know where Father is now

MOTHER
> (*In her own thoughts.*)
> On his ship I suppose

GIRL
> When is he coming home

MOTHER
> (*Still not completely with it.*)
> Could be a long time

GIRL
> You don't know

MOTHER
No how am I supposed to know that

GIRL
No

MOTHER
No how am I supposed to
(*Pause.*)
He hardly ever writes
Never telephones
he's out there
on some ship or other
I don't even know where he is
I don't know what the ship's name is

GIRL
He must have written it
(*Short pause.*)
He sends cards
He must have written it
in a card

MOTHER
The name of the ship

GIRL
Yes

MOTHER
Then
I've forgotten it

GIRL
I'm sure you have
(*Short pause.*)

MOTHER
He's been on so many ships

GIRL
He's been at sea for so long

MOTHER
As long as I've known him

GIRL
You married a seaman

MOTHER
I suppose I did

GIRL
D'you regret it

MOTHER
There's no point regretting

GIRL
But do you

MOTHER
Maybe
No what am I saying
Now and then
Maybe

GIRL
And you don't know where his ship is

MOTHER
No
how am I supposed to know that

GIRL
You don't know when he's coming home

MOTHER
No
Can't you talk about something else
(*Short pause.*)

GIRL
Like what
Tell me

MOTHER
Like the weather

GIRL
Like the weather

MOTHER
Yes like the weather

GIRL
It's raining of course like it always does

MOTHER
Not today

GIRL
It's not raining today

MOTHER
Yes it's raining
It's always raining

GIRL
Yes

MOTHER
That's how it is if you're a seaman

GIRL
Yes
(*Pause.*)
It's so long since he was home

MOTHER
Maybe a year
No not as long
half a year
maybe

GIRL
Yes

MOTHER
Yes something like that

GIRL
Yes then he must be coming home soon

MOTHER
Yes I'm sure he is

GIRL
> He will

MOTHER
> Yes

GIRL
> Yes
> (*Pause.*)
> And when he comes home
> he'll have such presents for us
> for you and for me
> and for my sister

MOTHER
> I'm sure he will

GIRL
> Bought in a far away country

MOTHER
> I'm sure he will have
> (*Pause.*)

GIRL
> Last time he came
> he brought that nice doll with him

MOTHER
> Yes it was nice
> But a doll
> for you
> you're almost grown up
> (*Short pause.*)
> But he doesn't think about that
> He still thinks you're a little girl
> he yes
> in actual fact you're
> a grown woman
> almost
> anyway

GIRL
>The doll was nice
>it was

MOTHER
>But imagine buying you a doll
>as if you were a little girl

GIRL
>And those nice lamps for the wall

MOTHER
>Yes

GIRL
>And the nice dresses

MOTHER
>Yes
>But of course they were
>(*Cuts herself off.*)

GIRL
>And the large trunk

MOTHER
>It's a long time since
>he brought that home
>(*Short pause.*)
>They all do that
>they buy trunks
>All seamen buy trunks
>you know

GIRL
>And he made a nice picture-frame

MOTHER
>Yes

GIRL
>Of empty cigarette packets

MOTHER
Yes

GIRL
Where your wedding picture is now

MOTHER
Yes yes

GIRL
Why do you say that
It's so nice
that picture

MOTHER
Very nice

GIRL
It's so long since the last time
he was home

MOTHER
Yes

GIRL
But he'll be home again soon

MOTHER
I've heard nothing from him

GIRL
You had a card

MOTHER
That was a long time ago

GIRL
Not that long ago

MOTHER
Quite a long time ago

GIRL
Only a week
something like that

MOTHER
A month easily

GIRL
Maybe a month

MOTHER
A month at least
(*Short pause.*)
But
I'd better go

GIRL
Where

MOTHER
I suppose I'll have to go shopping
We have to have food

GIRL
Yes

MOTHER
So I'll go shopping

GIRL
D'you know where my sister is

MOTHER
Asleep I suppose

GIRL
She came home late

MOTHER
I don't know

GIRL
She probably did

MOTHER
Maybe

GIRL
Did you come home late too

MOTHER
Don't ask like that
I'm your mother

GIRL
Yes

MOTHER
Mind your own business

GIRL
I was at home
I was the only one at home

MOTHER
And your sister

GIRL
I don't know where she was

MOTHER
She can't sit at home all the time either

GIRL
No
(*Pause.*)
Today
are you doing anything today

MOTHER
I
(*Cuts herself off.*)

GIRL
Town or anything

MOTHER
Maybe
yes
(*Short pause.*)
maybe I'll meet your uncle

GIRL
Our uncle
again

MOTHER
Maybe

GIRL
Today

MOTHER
Yes that's what I said

GIRL
You meet him nearly every day

MOTHER
He helps so much
we need a man
to help
and father

GIRL
(*Breaking in.*)
Yes

MOTHER
Yes well

GIRL
He may as well live here
Our uncle
(*Short pause.*)
Is he coming here
again today

MOTHER
Stop it now
Maybe
maybe he'll come
we haven't arranged anything
(*The MOTHER leaves. The WOMAN puts down her paintbrush,
watches her leave.*)

WOMAN
>Father was never there
>And Mother
>(*Short pause.*)
>was out every evening
>And Father never came home
>And I'd always be sitting there
>I'd always sit there
>on the sofa

GIRL
>I think I want to go into town

WOMAN
>And Mother
>(*Quite short pause.*)
>now she's old
>she's ill
>she's going to die

GIRL
>I can't just sit at home

WOMAN
>And Father's dead
>And our uncle's dead

GIRL
>I think I am good at drawing

WOMAN
>More and more often it was our uncle
>he came more and more often
>and then he was always there
>He just was there
>(*Short pause.*)
>And Father was never there
>that doll Father brought with him
>I was almost grown up

GIRL
>Maybe I can paint pictures

WOMAN
   I was almost grown up
   And Father came home with a doll
   And Mother thought
   it was so stupid
   And the doll
   she looked like
   yes like that girl
   (*Laughs a little.*)
   yes she looked a bit like that girl
   that I saw walking to school
   Or did she
   Maybe she didn't look like her
   But I think she did
   (*The WOMAN looks around.*)
   I'm a bit scared
   I'm often scared
   I don't know why I'm scared
   But I am scared
   (*Pause. The MAN comes in.*)

MAN
   Are you alright

WOMAN
   (*Smiles.*)
   Yes thank you

MAN
   You mean so much to me

WOMAN
   And you mean so much to me

MAN
   But you're so unhappy

WOMAN
   I'm happy enough

MAN
   Yes

WOMAN
It's true
(*Pause.*)

MAN
I have to go now
(*Quite short pause.*)
if I'm to get to work

WOMAN
Yes go

MAN
We'll talk later

WOMAN
Yes
Bye then
(*The MAN goes out and the MOTHER comes in wearing a dressing gown.*)

GIRL
(*To the MOTHER.*)
You aren't dressed yet

MOTHER
There's no rush
You aren't dressed either
so

GIRL
Mother
is my sister up

MOTHER
I don't know
(*Short pause.*)

GIRL
It got so late last night

MOTHER
I told you
I've just woken up

GIRL
Yes I heard
well
(*Short pause.*)
Mother
(*Short pause.*)
Mother

MOTHER
Yes what is it

GIRL
No nothing

MOTHER
Alright

GIRL
But

MOTHER
Yes

GIRL
You
Father
there was a card from him yesterday
Have you seen it
I left it on the kitchen table

MOTHER
Card from Father

GIRL
Yes

MOTHER
Sent from where

GIRL
Lisbon

MOTHER
Yes
well that's good
(*The MOTHER goes out. The GIRL and the WOMAN look
towards one another, then the WOMAN turns away.
Quite long pause.*)

WOMAN
And I see her before me now
(*Short pause.*)
Is there anything else like that
I remember
No
that's it
I don't think I remember anything else
I remember
(*Short pause.*)
I remember
yes
no it doesn't matter
Why do I remember of all things that Father sent cards
Maybe because it was me
who always got the post
Mother never got the post
for some reason or other she never did
Anyway
there was hardly ever any post
either
That's how it was
Cards from Father now and then
(*Quite short pause.*)
And we'd look at a globe
at where it'd come from
and wonder what the city was like
look at the sea
where the ship he was on
had sailed
those kind of things
But then

then it stopped being fun
Mother hardly looked at the cards he sent
let them just lie
threw them away
maybe
(*The MOTHER comes in, in her dressing gown.*)

GIRL
Will I get the card

MOTHER
If you like

GIRL
It's nice

MOTHER
I'm sure

GIRL
It's nice in Lisbon

MOTHER
The picture's of Lisbon

GIRL
Yes
(*Pause.*)

MOTHER
Your sister must be asleep

GIRL
I think so
(*Short pause.*)
But will

MOTHER
Yes

GIRL
Father
do you think he'll come home soon

MOTHER

What does he say

GIRL

I haven't read the card
it's for you
I don't read other people's post

MOTHER

It's probably for you too

GIRL

Maybe

MOTHER

Oh yes
of course

GIRL

Shall I get it

MOTHER

If you like
(*The GIRL remains seated and the MOTHER goes out. Quite long pause. The WOMAN looks around uncertainly and then moves forward decisively and the MAN enters and he walks after her.*)

MAN

Are you going to leave
(*The WOMAN stops.*)
Are you leaving

WOMAN

Yes

MAN

But
(*Short pause.*)
It would be good to see each other

WOMAN

I want to be on my own
(*Short pause.*)

But when I'm alone
it's good for a while
and then I feel
yes
despondent
it feels
as if no-one cares about me

MAN

But why can't we see each other

WOMAN

When I'm with someone
I want to be alone
My mother
she's ill
she's old
she's going to die
and I don't like her
I've never liked her
And she's never liked me
not from the moment she gave birth to me
She's always hated me
Why do I say things like this
Why do I use these words
What does it mean
when I say these words
What does it mean

MAN

We have to see each other

WOMAN

What does it mean
when I say that she hated me
It means nothing
Those words
Hated
Hated hate

MAN

> We can at least see each other
> can't we

WOMAN

> I can't be with anyone
> And I can't be alone
> I wasn't able to live with you
> That's how it was
> (*The MAN turns, goes out.*)
> They're there
> But I can't be with them
> I'm no longer where others are
> I'm another place
> I'm a place
> where no others are
> Where nobody is
> Where not even I am
> And then I think
> (*Laughs to herself.*)
> yes I think
> think and think
> I think
> yes
> yes for example
> yes that the only thing that's worth anything
> no
> no I don't know what's worth anything
> Because life's far too short
> (*Irritated with herself.*)
> Yes that's what I think
> that life is short
> What does that say
> Nothing
> It means nothing really
> That life's short
> it means that life is short
> short in relation to what
> to eternity

and of course life's too short
in relation to eternity
but then of course everything's too short
isn't it
and then
yes
in a way life is also an eternity
in relation to
yes to this eternity
It's not as eternal
and just as eternal
as everything else
yes
yes then
yes
yes then
(*The GIRL gets up and goes and looks at a photograph of
herself which is hanging on the wall, together with other family
photographs. She then looks at a photo of the FATHER standing
on the deck of a ship, she takes the photo down, stands looking
at it. The SISTER comes in, in a nightdress, looks towards the
GIRL, then goes and sits in an armchair, drawing her feet up
beneath her.*)

GIRL
    (*Half singing.*)
    Never ever again
    never ever again
    where are you father
    out there
    out there
    on all the world's oceans

SISTER
    Stop it

GIRL
    (*Continues.*)
    There on your oceans
    out there on your oceans

there on all the world's oceans
there on your oceans

SISTER
Stop it
I said

GIRL
Out there on the mighty ocean
on your mighty oceans

SISTER
Will you stop it _

GIRL
I have stopped

SISTER
Where's Mother

GIRL
How should I know

SISTER
You don't know

GIRL
She's not at home

SISTER
Tell me where she is

GIRL
She went out

SISTER
(*Questioning.*)
went out

GIRL
Yes out

SISTER
And you haven't seen her since

GIRL
No

SISTER
Is it long since she left

GIRL
Yes

SISTER
And she wasn't home last night

GIRL
I don't know

SISTER
You do know

GIRL
I went to bed

SISTER
But she wasn't at home when you went to bed

GIRL
I don't think so

SISTER
No of course she wasn't

GIRL
Where was she then

SISTER
How would I know

GIRL
Don't you

SISTER
No I don't

GIRL
She was probably with her lover I suppose

SISTER
Don't say things like that
She doesn't have a lover

GIRL
How do you know

SISTER
How can I know

GIRL
Why say it then

SISTER
I'm just saying it I suppose

GIRL
You don't know anything about it

SISTER
Yes

GIRL
No

SISTER
Yes

GIRL
What then

SISTER
Women need men

GIRL
She has a man

SISTER
But he's never home

GIRL
No

SISTER
Then does she have a man

GIRL
She has a man
and he
her man
is a seaman

and he's out there on all the world's oceans
(*Short pause.*)
and then he comes home
he comes home to her
to you
to me
to his women
he comes home
and he brings with him
such nice things

SISTER

He's coming home
when's he coming home

GIRL

He's coming home
Of course he must be
he sent a card
not so long ago

SISTER

He's hardly ever home
and he's got
a woman in every port
that's how it is
that's how it is when you're a seaman
seamen have women in every port
you must know that

GIRL

No

SISTER

Everyone says that

GIRL

Yes

SISTER

They say that seamen go to whores

GIRL
  Yes

SISTER
  They do

GIRL
  D'you believe
  father goes to whores

SISTER
  No

GIRL
  Yes you do
  You're just saying you don't

SISTER
  Then I do I suppose

GIRL
  You're mad
  Imagine thinking that
  I'd have thought
  (*Cuts herself off.*)

SISTER
  Yes

GIRL
  No nothing

SISTER
  Say it

GIRL
  No nothing

SISTER
  Say it

GIRL
  No

SISTER
  I know what you were going to say

GIRL
Yes

SISTER
That I
Yes I'm a bit of a whore myself

GIRL
No

SISTER
Don't lie

GIRL
Where were you last night

SISTER
Why are you asking that

GIRL
Just asking

SISTER
I was out

GIRL
But you came home so late

SISTER
Yes
aren't I allowed
what's it got to do with you
I come home when I want
I decide myself
You've got nothing to do with it

GIRL
No

SISTER
So why do you ask

GIRL
Nothing

SISTER
　Yes
　(*Short pause.*)
　just say it

GIRL
　Those clothes

SISTER
　Clothes

GIRL
　Yes those clothes

SISTER
　What clothes

GIRL
　You know which clothes I mean

SISTER
　I don't

GIRL
　Yes

SISTER
　No
　(*Pause.*)

GIRL
　You do know
　(*Pause.*)
　Those
　(*Short pause.*)
　those black ones

SISTER
　Have you been looking in my cupboard

GIRL
　No

SISTER
　Yes

GIRL
No I haven't

SISTER
You have
(*Short pause.*)
You mean the stockings
Those black stockings and the other things

GIRL
Yes
(*Short pause.*)
can I
try them
(*Quite short pause.*)
They look so
(*Cuts herself off.*)

SISTER
Stop it now

GIRL
And that sort of suspender belt thing
and the bra

SISTER
You've been looking in my cupboard

GIRL
Where did you get them from

SISTER
Bought them of course

GIRL
Do you use them

SISTER
I might

GIRL
When do you

SISTER
Don't ask so much

GIRL
> I'm just wondering

SISTER
> You're always wondering

GIRL
> Is that so strange
> is it
> (*Pause.*)
> D'you know where mother is

SISTER
> No I've said

GIRL
> You didn't say

SISTER
> I think she's out
> doing something or other
> I suppose she's doing something

GIRL
> I was just asking
> (*Pause.*)

SISTER
> Were you at home yesterday

GIRL
> Yes
> (*Pause.*)

SISTER
> Was our uncle here

GIRL
> Yes

SISTER
> A long time

GIRL
> Yes

(*Short pause.*)
I went to bed
so I don't really know
(*Short pause.*)
But he would've been gone when you came home
tell me where you were

SISTER
D'you have to know everything

GIRL
And you were wearing
(*Cuts herself off.*)

SISTER
You have to stop looking in my cupboard

GIRL
I haven't been looking

SISTER
How d'you know then

GIRL
How could I know
(*Short pause.*)
Why did you ask about our uncle

SISTER
I didn't ask about him

GIRL
No

SISTER
I think he was here last night

GIRL
No

SISTER
His shoes
his coat
were in the hall

GIRL
    Maybe
    (*Short pause.*)
    He is our uncle

SISTER
    Yes
    (*Pause.*)

GIRL
    Can I try
    (*Cuts herself off.*)

SISTER
    No

GIRL
    It's always no to me

SISTER
    Yes
    maybe
    another time

GIRL
    Now
    Straight away

SISTER
    No stop it

GIRL
    Yes
    Where are they

SISTER
    In my room
    of course

GIRL
    You'll let me try them
    then

SISTER
No
some other time
not now

GIRL
Yes

SISTER
You who won't even
tell me where Mother is

GIRL
What do you think

SISTER
I suppose she's gone shopping

GIRL
Yes maybe
(*Short pause.*)
or maybe she didn't come home last night
that could've happened

SISTER
And so it was only our uncle who was here

GIRL
It could've been
How would I know
(*Pause.*)
Aren't you going to get dressed soon

SISTER
Stop going on at me
You aren't even dressed yourself yet

GIRL
I'm not going on at you
I just asked

SISTER
Of course you're always
just asking
(*Pause.*)

GIRL
And what about him

SISTER
D'you have to start going on about him too
(*Pause.*)
Who do you mean anyway

GIRL
You must know

SISTER
Yes

GIRL
Yes him

SISTER
I don't understand what you're talking about

GIRL
Yes him

SISTER
Yes
(*Pause.*)

GIRL
Alright
I won't ask any more
I can't say anything
because whatever I say
is wrong
I can't say a single word
You always have to shout at me
And you've done that
since I was born
Mother told me that
that when I was little

before I could talk
or anything
when I was just lying there
you shouted at me then
said
No no
Naughty naughty
Bad girl
Even if I was just crawling around on the floor

SISTER
(*Cuts her off.*)
Yes yes

GIRL
(*Continues.*)
yes you shouted at me
you've never liked me
You've always thought I was just a nuisance
And I'm

SISTER
Not listening

GIRL
(*Continues.*)
I'm
your sister

SISTER
Stop it

GIRL
And you
you dress yourself up in those whore's stockings
there
And you think you look so gorgeous

SISTER
Stop it

GIRL
You put on make-up

until it runs
down your face
And then you walk around in those stockings there
With that black suspender belt
It looks so stupid
And if men

SISTER
(*Cuts her off.*)
What d'you know about men

GIRL
(*Continues.*)
if they think it's

SISTER
(*Cuts her off.*)
Don't talk about men

GIRL
No you're the one who can talk about them
(*Pause.*)
But
yes those clothes
yes
can I
(*Cuts herself off.*)

SISTER
If you want to so much
Yes alright then

GIRL
I want to
(*Pause.*)
can I

SISTER
Now straightaway

GIRL
Yes
can I

SISTER
I'll get no peace if you don't
alright

GIRL
Will you get them

SISTER
I suppose I'll have to
(*The SISTER goes out, the GIRL puts the photo back. Pause. The*
WOMAN and the GIRL look at each other. Pause. The SISTER
enters with a bundle of clothes.)
Here they are

GIRL
Let's see

SISTER
All yours
(*The SISTER lays the clothes on the table and the GIRL begins to*
pick them up. First, a pair of black net stockings.)

GIRL
These stockings
where did you get them

SISTER
Oh it's easy

GIRL
But where

SISTER
They sell them everywhere

GIRL
Not these
they can't

SISTER
Yes
just about

GIRL
No

SISTER
Don't keep saying that
Try them
put them on

GIRL
I don't know if I can

SISTER
It was you who wanted to
(*The GIRL picks up the suspender belt, holds it up in front of her.*)

GIRL
How can you wear things like this
(*The GIRL picks up the bra.*)
Completely see-through

SISTER
Your tits are too small

GIRL
Maybe

SISTER
But you can try if you want

GIRL
I don't think I do

SISTER
No alright
Alright then
Forget it
(*The GIRL picks up the short red patent leather skirt.*)

GIRL
God so sexy

SISTER
Stop it

GIRL
You can't go around in a skirt like that

SISTER
Yes I can

GIRL
No

SISTER
Yes

GIRL
No

SISTER
I can
because I do
You going to try them
or not

GIRL
Not when you're watching

SISTER
Don't be silly

GIRL
Alright then
(*The GIRL begins to pull on a stocking, she pulls on the second.
The SISTER stands and watches her, grins.*)
What is it

SISTER
Your knickers are ugly
Yes
They're completely wrong
Maybe you should try mine too
(*The GIRL puts on the suspender belt, tries to fasten the
stockings.*)
I'll help you
(*The SISTER fastens the stockings to the suspender belt, takes a
position and looks at the GIRL.*)
Oh yes now you're gorgeous
ha

(*The SISTER picks up the bra, holds it out.*)

GIRL
No
it's far too big

SISTER
Try it

GIRL
(*Takes it.*)
Alright then
(*The GIRL takes off her blouse and puts on the bra, it's far too big.*)

SISTER
Yes now you're gorgeous
ha
so gorgeous

GIRL
Don't be silly

SISTER
I'll get some make-up
(*The SISTER hurries out and the GIRL poses, pulls the briefs up further, tries to be as stylish as she can, then she takes the patent leather skirt, pulls it on. The WOMAN looks towards the GIRL, then looks down. The SISTER enters, carrying the doll the FATHER brought, holds it out to the GIRL.*)

GIRL
No

SISTER
Yes
you need to have the doll

GIRL
Don't mess around

SISTER
Yes

(*The GIRL takes the doll.*)

GIRL

I can't stand like this with a doll

SISTER

Sit down
(*The GIRL sits down with the doll in her lap and the SISTER
begins to make her up, she makes up her mouth completely red,
looks at her.*)
You're becoming completely irresistible now

GIRL

Don't say that

SISTER

And then we have to
(*Cuts herself off, begins to put colour on her eyelashes.*)
Like that yes
Let's have a look at you
Get up
(*The GIRL moves as if to put down the doll.*)
No you have to keep hold of the doll
you must understand that
you're my little sister aren't you
maybe

GIRL

No

SISTER

Yes
(*The GIRL gets up, stands there with the doll under her arm.*)
Go and look at yourself in the mirror
You're a real sight
(*The doorbell rings.*)

GIRL

(*Scared.*)
Somebody's here
You go
I have to take these clothes off

(The SISTER goes out and the GIRL picks up her blouse and she and the WOMAN look towards each other and the SISTER comes back in.)

SISTER
Hurry
He's coming

GIRL
Who

SISTER
Our uncle
of course
(The GIRL hurries out and the SISTER begins to collect up her make-up gear and the UNCLE enters.)

UNCLE
You're putting your make-up on

SISTER
Yes
Yes I should tidy up a bit
(Pause.)

UNCLE
Your mother's not home

SISTER
She's out shopping I suppose

UNCLE
Yes
And you're not dressed yet

SISTER
No
as you can see

UNCLE
Yes
(Short pause.)
yes I mean
it's late in the day
already

SISTER
Yes
(*Pause.*)

UNCLE
It's a while since I've seen you

SISTER
I guess

UNCLE
A few weeks
maybe

SISTER
Yes maybe a few weeks

UNCLE
Maybe longer
And everything's alright with you
(*Short pause.*)

SISTER
Yes

UNCLE
Good to hear

SISTER
Mother'll be coming soon
(*Short pause.*)

UNCLE
Have you heard anything from your father

SISTER
No
nothing

UNCLE
Not a thing

SISTER
No
(*Short pause.*)

It's a long time since he sent a card
He used to always send cards

UNCLE
Yes

SISTER
Must be several months since last time

UNCLE
Do you know where he is

SISTER
No

UNCLE
I see
(*The MOTHER comes in, wearing a coat, carrying two shopping bags.*)

MOTHER
(*To the UNCLE.*)
You're here

UNCLE
Yes
(*Pause.*)
yes shouldn't I be

MOTHER
yes of course
It's just so unexpected
in a way
(*The MOTHER looks towards the SISTER.*)
It's late
And you're not dressed yet
You can't go around like that

SISTER
No
(*Pause.*)

MOTHER

So go and get dressed then

(*The SISTER goes out and the MOTHER puts down the two shopping bags, she looks towards the UNCLE who goes over to her and puts his arms round her, she put her arms round him, they kiss. They sit on the sofa.*)

Oof yes

UNCLE

Maybe I shouldn't have come up here

MOTHER

Yes

Of course you should

(*The MOTHER leans against him and he kisses her again, she frees herself from him.*)

But

yes

yes she's home

UNCLE

She'll be getting dressed

MOTHER

Hope so

(*Long pause.*)

I'll take the shopping into the kitchen I suppose

UNCLE

Yes

but I can do it

MOTHER

No you sit

(*The GIRL comes in, in trousers and blouse.*)

You're home too

GIRL

I told you

I'm off school today

MOTHER

Yes maybe you did
(*The MOTHER looks towards the UNCLE.*)
Yes I forget almost everything

UNCLE

(*To the GIRL.*)
Yes
yes your mother needs a bit of help
with something
yes
so here I am
yes

GIRL

Yes
(*Short pause.*)

MOTHER

What do you look like
you've got make-up on

GIRL

Yes

MOTHER

You look terrible
(*The MOTHER gets up and the UNCLE gets up and takes the shopping bags and goes out.*)
Take that make-up off

GIRL

Yes

MOTHER

Yes
(*Pause.*)
What are you going to do today
now that you're off school
I mean

GIRL

I'm not sure

MOTHER

But why've you got so much make-up on

GIRL

I just put it on

MOTHER

Yes
(*Pause.*)
what're you going to do today
you didn't answer

GIRL

Go into town maybe

MOTHER

You should

GIRL

I think I will
(*The MOTHER goes out. Pause. The GIRL sits up in the corner
of the sofa with her feet drawn up. Quite long pause.*)

WOMAN

I paint
stupid pictures
I paint a picture of a girl on a sofa
And it becomes only a picture of the girl on the sofa
neither more nor less
Nothing else
Because I can't paint
(*Pause.*)
I haven't painted one good picture in the whole of my life
(*Short pause.*)
And it's true
(*Short pause.*)
because the most significant
insignificance
is always lacking

GIRL

I can't just stay home

I must do something
go into town
maybe

WOMAN
Now I'm trying to paint
a picture of a girl on a sofa
(*The WOMAN looks towards the GIRL.*)
and all it becomes is just
a picture of the girl on the sofa

GIRL
I'm good at drawing
Maybe I can paint pictures

WOMAN
I can't paint
(*Short pause.*)
because I paint only what I see
(*Pause.*)
But life can't be seen
(*Pause.*)
And those who can paint
they paint
(*Quite short pause.*)
yes the invisible
which is life
they paint life
where it disappears
(*Short pause.*)
and emerges_

GIRL
And our uncle's always here
And Father's never here
And my sister's at work
and then she goes out
in the evening

WOMAN
I can't paint

(*Short pause.*)
And now I've grown old
or almost old
And my sister's grown old too
And she's got herself a man and children
And a nice house

GIRL
I have to find something to do

WOMAN
And my sister's fine
(*Short pause.*)
And everything that's happened
is still present

GIRL
All I do is
sit here on the sofa

WOMAN
I just talk
I shouldn't open my mouth
(*Short pause.*)
But it's a bit like that
nevertheless
That everything that's been
is still present
without it being there

GIRL
I must want something
But I'm so bad at school

WOMAN
I always say
something or other
which is meant to sound
good
(*Short pause.*)
like the pictures too
in a way

should look good
so good
so nice
All it is is just colours
clinging colours
a heavy thing
amongst other heavy things
All the pictures I've painted
How heavy they are
Heavy from the colours
I'm not even able to move them
All they are is weight

GIRL
I think I'll go into town today
I'm off school

WOMAN
The pictures are just things
heavy things
which must be thrown away
since no-one wants
what I paint
(*Quite short pause.*)
They don't have the space
(*Quite short pause.*)
The pictures are too big

GIRL
I'm good at drawing
Maybe I can paint pictures

WOMAN
I paint badly
I can't paint
(*Pause.*)
I want to paint Mother out

GIRL
(*Looks at the WOMAN, questioning.*)
Paint Mother out

WOMAN
(*Looks at the GIRL, then looks away.*)
I want to paint Mother out
(*Short pause.*)
because of course she wants everything to be so good
And of course I want everything to be so good
like Mother always wanted it to be
everything to be so good
light and easy
like a sunny summer's day
yellow and white
nice
That's how it was to be
light
and yellow and nice and light and easy
And pink
And lace trim
And black

GIRL
I can't just sit here

WOMAN
And yellow
most of all yellow
she wanted it to be
yellow
yellow as the sun
Nothing else
just yellow
(*Short pause.*)
And Mother would walk around
in a pink nightdress
her breasts moving from side to side
how could Father stand it

GIRL
Father's never at home

WOMAN
He couldn't stand it

either
he travelled
or he didn't come home
he stayed out there at sea
on the ocean
or wherever he was
the seaman
He came home
stayed a while
and then he was off again
disappeared
Out the door
And that was him gone

GIRL
I can't just sit here
(*Short pause.*)

WOMAN
There's nothing more to remember
I'm sure
there's nothing more I really want to remember
(*Hesitates.*)
Everything I say
isn't worth saying

GIRL
I think I'll go into town

WOMAN
And what I say
of course means nothing

GIRL
I can't just stay here
(*The SISTER comes in, dressed in net stockings and the patent leather skirt, high-heeled boots. To the SISTER.*)
You've dressed up

SISTER
Yes

GIRL
  Have you got all of it on
  (*The WOMAN picks up a paintbrush, begins to paint a black
  suspender belt on the GIRL.*)

SISTER
  Yes

GIRL
  Everything
  the suspender belt too

SISTER
  Yes

GIRL
  I don't believe it

SISTER
  You want to see

GIRL
  No

SISTER
  Yes you do
  (*The SISTER loosens the leather skirt and it falls to the floor and
  stands there in the net stockings held up with a suspender belt.*)

GIRL
  You look like a whore

SISTER
  Men like it

GIRL
  Yes that's why
  Have you got the see-through bra on

SISTER
  Yes
  (*The SISTER unbuttons her blouse.*)

GIRL
  Stop it

SISTER
Didn't you have it on earlier

GIRL
Yes

SISTER
Yes exactly

GIRL
Where are you going

SISTER
Wouldn't you like to know

GIRL
No
(*Short pause.*)
Are you going to meet someone

SISTER
I suppose I am

GIRL
A man

SISTER
I suppose I am

GIRL
Do you
(*Short pause.*)
when
do you do dirty things together

SISTER
Wouldn't you like to know

GIRL
Where are you going to meet him

SISTER
He's picking me up

GIRL
He has a car

SISTER
  Yes

GIRL
  Do you do dirty things in his car

SISTER
  Stop asking me
  (*The SISTER pulls up the patent leather skirt, does it up.*)

GIRL
  I think you do dirty things

SISTER
  Maybe

GIRL
  In his car

SISTER
  I wouldn't think about it too much
  (*The SISTER does up her blouse.*)
  I'm going

GIRL
  Yes

SISTER
  Bye
  (*The SISTER goes, stops suddenly and stands looking at the
  SISTER OLDER, who enters walking towards her and who
  walks on further towards the WOMAN, who sees her coming, but
  pretends that she doesn't, plays ignorant, while the SISTER goes
  out, goes away from the picture and from the SISTER OLDER.*)

 SISTER OLDER
  (*To the WOMAN.*)
  We were going to go together and visit Mother
  And you didn't come

WOMAN
  (*Stops, turns to the SISTER OLDER.*)
  No

SISTER OLDER
>We agreed to meet each other
>at the Nursing home
>we were going to visit her
>(*The WOMAN goes towards the picture of the girl on the sofa,*
>*as if she's unaware that the SISTER OLDER is talking to her,*
>*begins to paint black net stockings on the GIRL.*)
>We did didn't we
>Today
>we were going to go today
>You and me
>We're sisters aren't we
>We're her daughters
>The only thing she has in life
>(*Short pause.*)
>I've been there several times
>and visited her
>but you
>it's such a long time since you've been there
>You must come
>you have to
>for Mother's sake
>She's sick
>she may die
>why don't you like her
>why've you never liked her
>but now
>now Mother is sick
>(*Short pause.*)
>can't you make your peace with her
>you should do it
>(*Short pause.*)
>before it's too late
>(*The WOMAN walks back and stands and looks at the picture,*
>*then turns, looks round and stands looking at the FATHER*
>*OLDER, who comes walking towards her.*)

WOMAN
>Father
>it's so good to see you again

I hardly ever see you

FATHER OLDER
Well you know
I'm not well
And I prefer to stay at home

WOMAN
Some home
(*Cuts herself off.*)

FATHER OLDER
It's alright
there

WOMAN
You never complain

FATHER OLDER
It doesn't help hato complain
(*Pause.*)
You're alright

WOMAN
Yes
I suppose I am
(*Pause.*)

FATHER OLDER
You and him
you haven't moved back in together

WOMAN
No
It's better for me to be alone

FATHER OLDER
I can understand that
yes

WOMAN
You'd know

FATHER OLDER
I suppose I do

WOMAN
Yes
(*The FATHER OLDER looks down, goes into himself, then leaves. The WOMAN puts down her paintbrush. Pause. The SISTER OLDER and the WOMAN look towards each other. Long pause.*)

SISTER OLDER
(*Hesitant.*)
But
when Father was alive
while he was alive
you went and visited him
That's how it always was
you and Father
and me and Mother
How did it get like that

WOMAN
Mother never liked me

SISTER OLDER
It was you who didn't like her
That's what you're always saying

WOMAN
But it's true

SISTER OLDER
It's not true
She liked you
And besides
yes
now she's old
she might die any day

WOMAN
Mother never liked me
I liked her
all my life I liked her
from the time I was born
I liked her so much

and I did everything I could
to make her like me
Everything
I
Yes
Everything
(*Short pause.*)
But she didn't like me
And then
yes
it went on so long
I just stopped trying

SISTER OLDER
And you stopped visiting her

WOMAN
Yes

SISTER OLDER
There were so many years
when you hardly saw each other

WOMAN
I didn't want to see her

SISTER OLDER
But you visited Father

WOMAN
Yes yes
yes Father and me
yes
he had no-one else
He sat there in his room
at that Seaman's home
sat there alone
he had almost nothing
he sat there and rolled his cigarettes
went to that dingy café
and drank a few glasses of beer
went back to his room

It was only me who visited him

SISTER OLDER

I couldn't stand seeing him sitting there
His stubble
the smell of smoke
He hardly ever washed himself
(*Laughs briefly.*)
didn't wash himself
or his room
And those yellow brown fingers
Roll-ups the whole time
And if he said anything
yes it was always the same
the same things about the different ships
he'd been on
and said something
something about how he'd met someone or other
who he'd been on a ship with
at some time or another

WOMAN

Yes

SISTER OLDER

He went with whores
I'm sure about that

WOMAN

He was your Father

SISTER OLDER

I'm sure he was

WOMAN

You don't think he was

SISTER OLDER

I'm sure he was my Father

WOMAN

You look like him

SISTER OLDER
Maybe a bit
(*Short pause.*)
You're not coming to see Mother

WOMAN
No

SISTER OLDER
But it's true
she's in a bad way
they rang from the Nursing home
she
yes
yes they asked me to come
you must come

WOMAN
She doesn't like me
It's best
for her
that I don't come

SISTER OLDER
She likes you
She always asks after you
She misses you
I know she does
And now
(*Short pause.*)
yes you
you're going to regret it
if she dies now
Yes
yes I know it
For your own sake you have to come with me
She likes you
She always has
You just misunderstand

WOMAN
    You've said that before

SISTER OLDER
    It's true

WOMAN
    She's never

SISTER OLDER
    (*Cuts her off.*)
    Stop it
    It's not the time for it
    We have to go
    They rang from the nursing home
    Mother isn't well
    we have to go
    we can't stand here like this
    I have to go there
    whatever happens
    And you should come too
    We should go together
    We're her daughters
    We're all she has
    She's alone
    She's going to die
    We have to go

WOMAN
    I don't want to
    I'm not going to

SISTER OLDER
    You have to

WOMAN
    She left me
    And I left her

SISTER OLDER
    You keep saying that
    Mother

(*Hesitates.*)
what was she supposed to do
There was nothing else she could do

WOMAN
No
maybe not
You go
You should go
She
(*Cuts herself off.*)

SISTER OLDER
I don't understand you

WOMAN
Go now

SISTER OLDER
Alright
(*Short pause.*)
But you're going to regret it
I know it
You don't know what you're doing
It's your decision
(*The SISTER OLDER goes out and the WOMAN goes over to
the picture of the girl on the sofa, looks at it, then turns and sees
the MOTHER come in, dressed in skirt and blouse, and then the
UNCLE comes in after her.*)

UNCLE
You're looking lovely

MOTHER
Do you think so

UNCLE
Yes very nice

MOTHER
Thank you

UNCLE

You look so nice
that I
yes I
(*The UNCLE goes over and puts his arms around the MOTHER
from behind and presses her against him, he kisses her on the
cheek, she turns, they kiss each other a long time.*)
I get so
I start to
Can't we
yes
now
yes straight away

MOTHER

But we can't
(*Cuts herself off.*)
They could be
(*Cuts herself off.*)

UNCLE

They're not at home
Let's do it
Here
On the floor

MOTHER

No

UNCLE

Yes
(*The UNCLE feels her breasts, first over her blouse, then he puts
his hands underneath it.*)
Now
I want you
Now
Straight away

MOTHER

But what if

UNCLE
No-one's home
(*Short pause.*)
Or we
yes
yes we can go into the bathroom

MOTHER
Maybe
(*The UNCLE kisses her. The MOTHER frees herself.*)
No we can't
It's morning
Not now

UNCLE
But

MOTHER
(*As if talking strictly to a child.*)
No no
Later
not now

UNCLE
(*A little put out.*)
Alright
(*Pause.*)
Is he coming back soon

MOTHER
I think so
Or maybe not
(*Short pause.*)
I just got a card from him

UNCLE
Yes from some place or other

MOTHER
Yes I don't remember

UNCLE
It's a long time since he was last home

MOTHER
A couple of years
no not so long
I
(*Laughs briefly.*)
no I don't remember
(*The MOTHER kisses the UNCLE on the cheek.*)

UNCLE
But he's coming home soon

MOTHER
Yes he has to

UNCLE
And what then

MOTHER
I've no idea
(*Short pause.*)
why do you have to be his brother
It makes everything so much worse

UNCLE
I can't help it
that's what I am
There's nothing we can do about it
that's how it's turned out
(*Pause.*)

MOTHER
Yes
(*Pause.*)
Should I write to him
about us

UNCLE
No you mustn't
You can't
No not that
It
(*Cuts himself off.*)

No
(*Pause. The GIRL gets up from the sofa where she's been sitting the whole time and walks out on to the floor.*)

MOTHER
(*To the GIRL.*)
You're not at school

GIRL
I'm off
I said that
I told you

UNCLE
(*To the GIRL.*)
Hello

GIRL
Hello

MOTHER
And you
what're you doing today

GIRL
I don't know

MOTHER
You're not playing truant I hope

GIRL
Why d'you say that
I told you I've got the day off
I do get days off school

MOTHER
Yes I didn't mean it that way
(*Short pause.*)
and actually
when I think about it
you did tell me
you did say you'd the day off today
(*Laughs briefly.*)

I don't remember anything
but
yes

UNCLE

Yes she did say that
I remember
She did say she'd have the day off today
that's right

GIRL

I'm going for a walk
into town

MOTHER

Yes do
And your Sister

GIRL

At work
(*The MOTHER and the UNCLE sit on the sofa, and the GIRL goes over to the WOMAN, takes a position next to her. Quite long pause. The UNCLE puts his arm around the MOTHER's shoulders. Pause.*)

MOTHER

Why doesn't he write
letters
I mean
or ring
Just those cards

UNCLE

He's always been like that

MOTHER

Always

UNCLE

Yes

MOTHER

You know him better
than me

UNCLE
    Yes and no

MOTHER
    You grew up together
    you and him

UNCLE
    Yes we did
    Can't deny that

MOTHER
    You were never good friends

UNCLE
    No
    (*Pause.*)

MOTHER
    I suppose brothers
    don't always have to be good friends

UNCLE
    It can happen
    (*Pause.*)
    How long's it been since you heard from him

MOTHER
    I'm not sure

UNCLE
    I suppose he'll send a card
    soon
    you'll see

MOTHER
    Yes

UNCLE
    And he'll phone one day

MOTHER
    I suppose he might
    (*The MOTHER laughs briefly.*)

UNCLE
>   That's how it is
>   for a seaman
>   You know
>   yes you can't think about too much
>   about those back home
>   it can be painful
>   that
>   those who think too much about their wife and children
>   they can't settle
>   they can't sleep
>   they sit and stare
>   at the waves
>   on the ocean
>   they can't cope
>   they begin to drink too much
>   they get scared
>   of being alone
>   that they'll lose their sanity
>   and jump into the ocean
>   yes it happens a lot

MOTHER
>   Don't talk like that

UNCLE
>   It happens
>   It's not uncommon
>   In the dark night
>   as the ship works and works its way forward
>   over the black ocean
>   under the black sky
>   they go out
>   and stand in the darkness
>   holding onto the rail
>   And between the man standing there
>   and the enormous darkness
>   is only that rail
>   some rusting iron pipes welded together
>   painted white

MOTHER
  You can't say this
  Think about us
  about me

UNCLE
  And the engine which keeps turning

MOTHER
  (*Continues.*)
  think about us at home
  yes about us
  what about us
  It's not so easy for us
  either

UNCLE
  No
  But he has to
  I'm just trying to say that he
  he can't think about you too often
  that's how it is with a seaman
  to be out there on all the world's oceans
  to have to stay there
  to have to do your work
  Then to have to come home again
  to the wife
  to the children
  to the daughters

MOTHER
  After having had
  a woman in every port

UNCLE
  Yes

MOTHER
  You think so

UNCLE
  That's what it's like

MOTHER
    Are you sure

UNCLE
    They say that
    that it's like that

MOTHER
    But what about me

UNCLE
    You

MOTHER
    Yes
    while he
    in every port
    so I sit
    at home
    trying to bring up two daughters
    the best I can
    and then he's doing
    yes
    (*Cuts herself off.*)

UNCLE
    Don't think about it
    You shouldn't think about
    There's so much in life you shouldn't see
    And so much
    you shouldn't think about
    if you're to cope
    so

MOTHER
    I can't let it go

UNCLE
    No

MOTHER
    I can't cope with it
    And I

am I not a beautiful woman
(*Laughs a little, and puts it on a bit.*)
attractive
just look
yes even though I've almost full-grown
daughters

MOTHER
am I not
yes quite
yes attractive

UNCLE
You are

MOTHER
But look

UNCLE
Yes

MOTHER
Aren't I

UNCLE
Yes

MOTHER
And I'm here just wasting away

UNCLE
You're looking after your daughters

MOTHER
They're almost grown up

UNCLE
You've got two lovely daughters

MOTHER
You think so

UNCLE
Yes

MOTHER
Yes
(*Pause.*)

UNCLE
And he sends money

MOTHER
Money comes every month

UNCLE
You don't do too
(*Cuts himself off.*)

MOTHER
I don't do too well either

UNCLE
Well who does

MOTHER
No that's true

UNCLE
Yes
(*Pause.*)

MOTHER
You're alright

UNCLE
Getting by

MOTHER
It's the same for you
as

UNCLE
(*Cuts in.*)
Yes
(*The UNCLE puts his arms around her, kisses her and they lie on the sofa, lie and hold each other. Short pause. The WOMAN sees the FATHER OLDER come in and walks towards him.*)

WOMAN
Father
It's so good to see you
But you look
You should
(*Cuts herself off.*)
No I won't say anything
It's good to see you
It's nice you've come

FATHER OLDER
Yes thanks for phoning
and asking me

WOMAN
We hardly ever see each other

FATHER OLDER
Yes
you're right
(*The MAN comes in. The FATHER OLDER moves away from
the WOMAN, takes a position, looks down.*)

MAN
(*To the WOMAN.*)
I have to talk to you

WOMAN
It's no good talking

MAN
I need you

WOMAN
It's no good
We've talked and talked
(*Short pause.*)
There's nothing more to say

MAN
Just talk with me

WOMAN
  There's nothing more to say

MAN
  No

WOMAN
  Everything's been said

MAN
  But

WOMAN
  There's nothing more to say

MAN
  What have I done wrong

WOMAN
  It's not like that

MAN
  What is it
  (*Short pause.*)
  When I grew up

WOMAN
  (*Cuts him off.*)
  Yes I know
  You've told me so many times

MAN
  D'you want me to leave
  (*The WOMAN shrugs her shoulders. Pause.*)

WOMAN
  You haven't done anything wrong

MAN
  But you don't want to be with me any more

WOMAN
  No
  I want to be on my own
  (*The MAN leaves. Quite long pause. The WOMAN and the*

*FATHER OLDER look shyly towards each other, he then looks
down, stands completely stiffly, with his eyes fixed down at an
angle.)*
No
(*Pause.*)
Everyone who's been here
Everything that's happened
(*The WOMAN goes over and strokes the face of the FATHER
OLDER.*)
And Father
Dear Father
I wish you'd lived longer
you sat there in the Seaman's home
and went out in the morning
for a few glasses of beer
then went back again
The days passed
they became
a few years
and then you were gone
Dear Father
(*Pause.*)
And I did come to visit you
in your room
at the Seaman's home
(*The FATHER OLDER goes out, and the MOTHER gets up
from the sofa, walks out onto the floor, takes a position, resting
on one leg and the UNCLE gets up, goes over to the MOTHER,
unbuttons her blouse, takes it off, then he takes off his shirt, goes
behind the MOTHER, holds her, first around the stomach, then
her breasts, he touches her breasts and she leans against him,
they kiss. The WOMAN stands watching, she becomes more and
more embarassed; she becomes like a child in the face, and the
GIRL looks towards the WOMAN, also embarassed, a bit giggly,
then they both turn away but are curious, so they watch again,
look down, not knowing quite what to do with themselves and
the UNCLE presses the MOTHER into him, kisses her for a
long time, then he loosens her skirt, it falls to the floor and the
MOTHER is standing there in brown tights and the UNCLE*

fondles her bottom with both hands, they lie down on the floor, he lies on top of her.)

MOTHER
(*A little breathless.*)
But not
I'm not sure if
My daughters

UNCLE
They're not at home

MOTHER
(*Turns away.*)
Someone might come
(*The UNCLE lies on top of her again, kisses her, and then the FATHER walks in very slowly, he stops, looks towards the MOTHER and the UNCLE. Very long pause. The MOTHER sits up slowly. To the FATHER, scared.*)
Have you come
(*Pause.*)
home now
(*Pause.*)
then
(*Cuts herself off. The FATHER stands calmly and looks towards the MOTHER, who gets up while the UNCLE remains sitting on the floor. The FATHER just looks at them, then turns.*)
But
(*Pause.*)
is it you
or
you
I
are you here
But
(*The FATHER starts to leave slowly and the UNCLE gets up and the MOTHER looks at the FATHER leaving.*)
But
yes
I don't understand

(*Pause.*)
Are you going to leave again straight away
(*The FATHER leaves. Calls after him.*)
You've just arrived
so out of the blue
(*The UNCLE rebuttons his shirt.*)
I didn't know
But
you

WOMAN
(*Stands completely calm.*)
Father
It's so long since I've seen you
Where have you come from

GIRL
And you mustn't leave again
you mustn't leave straight away
Father
come back

WOMAN
Don't leave
I've been waiting for you
This is stupid

GIRL
You can't just leave

WOMAN
Father
Where are you
Don't say anything
(*Quite long pause. The WOMAN walks forward a little, looks towards the MOTHER and the UNCLE who stand looking uncomprehending towards each other. Pause.*)

UNCLE
It's not possible

MOTHER
It can't be real

UNCLE
He was just standing there all of a sudden

MOTHER
It's unbelievable
It's not possible
It's just stupid
(*The MOTHER laughs.*)

UNCLE
He came
He stood there
Like that
Just now
It happened just now

MOTHER
These things don't happen

UNCLE
Was he not
on a ship
some far away place or other

MOTHER
Yes
(*The MOTHER and the UNCLE look towards each other for a
long time, then they laugh and then go out, first the MOTHER
and then the UNCLE and at the same time the FATHER
OLDER comes in.*)

WOMAN
And he never came back
Father never came back
He sent letters
(*The FATHER OLDER walks towards the WOMAN.*)
asked if he could meet me
my sister

WOMAN
(*To the FATHER OLDER.*)
Father
You just left

FATHER OLDER
> I had to

WOMAN
> You never saw Mother again

FATHER OLDER
> I couldn't
> I never wanted to see her
> not after that
> And I never did

WOMAN
> You were never divorced

FATHER OLDER
> I didn't want to see her

WOMAN
> Never

FATHER OLDER
> I never wanted to see her again
> And I never saw her again

WOMAN
> Now Mother's old
> She's going to die

FATHER OLDER
> I never wanted to see her again
> (*The MOTHER comes in, in a dress suit, she stops, as if she is*
> *waiting for somebody to come, but nobody comes, she gets a little*
> *disappointed takes a position and stands as if in her own thoughts*
> *and then, after a while, the UNCLE enters and the FATHER*
> *OLDER goes out. Quite long pause.*)

SISTER OLDER
> (*Comes in.*)
> It's over
> Mother's dead
> She died tonight

WOMAN
    Mother's dead

SISTER OLDER
    She died tonight

WOMAN
    She's dead

SISTER OLDER
    It was going to happen
    she'd been sick for a long time

WOMAN
    No

SISTER OLDER
    But now it's over

WOMAN
    Were you there

SISTER OLDER
    Yes
    or
    yes they rang
    and I went as quickly as I could

WOMAN
    Did you talk to her

SISTER OLDER
    No
    she couldn't talk
    she just lay there
    didn't say anything
    just lay there

WOMAN
    Did she

SISTER OLDER
    Now she's dead
    And we have to

WOMAN
> (*Continues.*)
> arrange the funeral

SISTER OLDER
> I suppose we have to

WOMAN
> Yes
> (*The SISTER OLDER goes out, and the WOMAN looks towards the MOTHER who walks over to the UNCLE and leans into him, and he puts his arms around her, presses her towards him. The WOMAN looks away from them. To herself.*)
> I tell myself that here is where we are
> Here
> Now
> Just now
> Just here
> (*Short pause.*)
> And here
> (*Short pause.*)
> here's where we're going to be
> for quite a long time

GIRL
> a very long time

WOMAN
> incredibly long
> (*Short pause.*)
> or maybe not
> maybe we aren't going to be here
> (*Short pause.*)
> but a totally different place
> where it's quite different
> (*Short pause.*)
> I don't know

GIRL
> I don't know anything

WOMAN
I don't know this
or anything else
or anything

GIRL
Nothing

WOMAN
Not a single thing in the world
Nothing
(*Short pause.*)
But it should be quiet
in the song
(*Thinks.*)
yes in the song
quiet

GIRL
so quiet

WOMAN
as quiet as an old day
(*Short pause.*)
So let it fade away
let it then come
let it then become
let it then be there
let it stay
let it stay there
let it stay there
and then
(*Cuts herself off. The WOMAN looks, takes a paintbrush and goes over to the picture of the girl on the sofa and paints across it, over it in black.*)
I can't paint
And I don't want to paint any more
(*Pause.*)
So now the girl on the sofa will have gone

(*The GIRL goes and sits in the corner of the sofa with her feet drawn up.*)
I can't paint things out
(*Quite short pause.*)
they're always there
Therefore I can't paint
(*Quite short pause. The WOMAN moves away from the picture and the MAN comes walking towards her and she walks towards him.*)

MAN

It was good to see you again

WOMAN

Yes
(*Short pause.*)
I just thought
it would be good to meet up
That's why I rang
It's been so long since last time

MAN

Yes it has been

WOMAN

You don't have to
meet me
if you don't want to
so

MAN

I'm alright now

WOMAN

Yes

MAN

We're happy together
Her and me

WOMAN

You and her
yes her

your new woman
you're happy together

MAN
Yes
(*Pause.*)
And you

WOMAN
Mother's dead

MAN
Yes I heard

WOMAN
Good to see you again

MAN
Yes it was good to see you
(*The WOMAN and the MAN look towards each other, then they
walk away from each other.*)

WOMAN
(*After the MAN, who walks away and out.*)
But don't leave
Because then
(*Short pause.*)
because then
then I'll be completely alone
in the mornings
why should I get up

GIRL
I'm so alone
so alone that I haven't a face

WOMAN
I haven't a face
I can't see
there's not anything in me
to make me see
I don't have
(*Cuts herself off.*)

GIRL
I don't want to go out

WOMAN
And there's no-one else
only
(*Laughs briefly.*)
myself
and what's that
Something which sits here

GIRL
I'm not anything
just something which sits here

WOMAN
(*After the MAN, who has gone.*)
No don't go
No
because then
(*Cuts herself off. Pause.*)
No nothing
I can't do anything else
I haven't done anything else
And I'm not painting any more

SISTER
(*Comes in, wearing the net stockings, the patent leather skirt, high-heeled boots.*)
I'm going

GIRL
Where

SISTER
Out

GIRL
But where

SISTER
D'you have to know

GIRL
> No
> (*Pause.*)
> Yes you just go
> what're you waiting for

SISTER
> I just thought I'd tell you

GIRL
> Yes thanks

SISTER
> D'you know where Mother is

GIRL
> I've no idea

SISTER
> D'you know what time she went out

GIRL
> No

SISTER
> Alright then

GIRL
> You should go

SISTER
> Yes I'm going
> (*The WOMAN goes and sits in the right-hand corner of the sofa, also with her feet drawn up. The GIRL and the WOMAN look at each other.*)

> *Blackout.*

Printed in the USA
CPSIA information can be obtained
at www.ICGtesting.com
LVHW020855171024
794056LV00002B/547